Dag Hewa

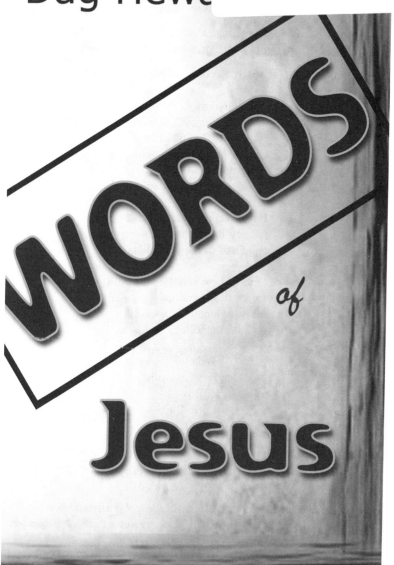

WORDS

of

Jesus

Unless otherwise stated, all Scripture quotations are taken from the King James Version of the Bible.

Excerpts in Chapter 3, from *Evidence that Demands a Verdict*, by Josh McDowell, pg. 129-131. Used by permission of Thomas Nelson Publishers.

Excerpt in Chapter 13, from *Snakes in the Lobby* by Scott MacLeod, pg. 13-22. Copyright: Scott MacLeod. Used by Permission.

Poem in Chapter 15, by Gordon Lindsay. Source Unknown.

E mail Dag Heward-Mills :
bishop@daghewardmills.org
evangelist@daghewardmills.org

Find out more about Dag Heward-Mills at:
www.daghewardmills.org
www.lighthousechapel.org
www.healingjesuscrusade.org

Write to:
Dag Heward-Mills
P.O. Box 114
Korle-Bu
Accra
Ghana

ISBN 13: 978-0-7963-0807-8

Dedication

To my mother, *Mrs. Elisabeth Heward-Mills*
You raised me. You have loved and supported me in varied
ways all these years, and still do. Thank you.

From a grateful son.

Contents

Chapter 1

The Power and the Beauty of Our Lord's Words

It is enough to place the words of Jesus above all human words. We only need to know for certain what Jesus believed in, in order to believe the same.

Today, the words of Jesus are separated from the rest of scripture by red ink.

Formerly, the beautiful words of Christ were indiscriminately mingled with the rest of Scripture. Modern Bibles assign the deserved honour to these timeless words. They are placed in a class of their own. A class without equal.

At the Reformation, men focused on the work of Christ on Calvary. Later, the person of Christ was the focus of attention. In later years, the details of *His earthly life* from the manger to the cross became the focus of intense study.

However, I believe that the hour has come when *His words* will be the focus of attention. A study of the earthly life and the works of Christ are different from a study of the words of Christ.

The church today has in them, more of the Pauline epistles than the gospels. As the end approaches His words will take pre-eminence in the church. Saint Paul must be read in the light of Christ rather than Christ in the light of Saint Paul.

Fortunately, the unique value of the words of Jesus is being recognized. At last, these words have been assigned the distinction and the commanding authority they deserve. As someone said, Jesus is the best teacher of His own religion.

The brief commands that pronounced healing on numerous sick bodies leave the reader in awe of the Saviour.

The sentences from the Sermon on the Mount have found a lodgment in the memories of all Christians.

The parables of Jesus have never failed to charm their readers.

The farewell discourses recorded in the book of John have in every generation been the guidance and consolation of the Church.

The rambling stories of Jesus are unforgettable and unrivaled.

Truly, the power and beauty of the words of Jesus are cherished by all and sundry.

Chapter 2

What Jesus Said About His Own Words

1. Jesus taught that words in general are not trivial things.

Jesus took a very high and unusual view of the value of words in general. There is nothing that appears more trivial to the ordinary man than a word. No, said Jesus, it does not end there, and it does not end ever. Words are not trivial. When they are called into existence they become living things which travel through time and space, doing good and evil; and they will confront us again at the last day.

But I say unto you, That every idle word that men shall speak, they shall give account thereof in the day of judgment.

Matthew 12:36

2. Jesus taught that words would be used as a basis for judgment.

The influence of our words on our destiny will be extraordinary; "...for by thy words thou shalt be justified and by thy words, thou shall be condemned" (Matthew 12:37).

There is nothing of which the average man is more surely convinced than that his tongue is his own, and that he can at will make it utter words either good or evil.

3. Jesus taught that words were the unmistakable portrayal of a person.

If the speaker be good, then his words are good, but if the speaker be evil, then they are inevitably evil.

O generation of vipers, how can ye, being evil, speak good things? for out of the abundance of the heart the mouth speaketh.

Matthew 12:34

A man cannot alter the character of his words unless he first alters his own nature. For out of the abundance of the heart, the mouth speaks. Such was Christ's concept of words, and such were His own words. They were the overflowings of His very heart.

4.   **Jesus declared in sober earnest that His words would outlast the created heavens and earth.**

Heaven and earth shall pass away: but my words shall not pass away.

Luke 21:33

Poets and thinkers have sometimes boasted that their words would survive the most permanent works of man such as pyramids and monuments. But Jesus declared that His words would outlast the most stable works of God.

5.   **Jesus spoke of the attachment to His words as the sign of attachment to Himself. Jesus considered devotion to His words to be the test of discipleship.**

If you continue in my words then are you my disciples. You will know the truth and the truth will make you free.

Then said Jesus to those Jews which believed on him, If ye continue in my word, then are ye my disciples indeed;

John 8:31

Jesus answered and said unto him, If a man love me, he will keep my words: and my Father will love him, and we will come unto him, and make our abode with him. He that loveth me not keepeth not my sayings: and the word which ye hear is not mine, but the Father's which sent me.

John 14:23-24

6.   When Mary was seated at his feet listening to His Words, He declared that she was doing the one thing that was needful.

But one thing is needful: and Mary hath chosen that good part, which shall not be taken away from her

Luke 10:42

7.   Jesus attributed to His words the power of cleansing the heart.

Now ye are clean through the word which I have spoken unto you (John 15:3). Verily, verily, I say unto you, If a man keep my saying, he shall never see death. (John 8:51) It is the spirit that quickeneth; the flesh profiteth nothing: the words that I speak unto you, they are spirit, and they are life (John 6:63). Then Simon Peter answered him, Lord, to whom shall we go? Thou hast the words of eternal life. (John 6:68)

8.   Jesus alleged that the eternal destiny of His hearers would depend on the attitude they assumed to His words.

He that rejecteth me, and receiveth not my words, hath one that judgeth him: the word that I have spoken, the same shall judge him in the last day.

John 12:48

Therefore whosoever heareth these sayings of mine, and doeth them, I will liken him unto a wise man, which built his house upon a rock: And the rain descended, and the floods came, and the winds blew,

and beat upon that house; and it fell not: for it was founded upon a rock. And every one that he areth these sayings of mine, and doeth them not, shall be likened unto a foolish man, which built his house upon the sand: And the rain descended, and the floods came, and the winds blew, and beat upon that house; and it fell: and great was the fall of it.

Matthew 7:24-27

Chapter 3

What Others Said about the Words of Jesus

… Never man spake like this man.

John 7:46

…What a Word is this!…….

Luke 4:36

The words of Jesus are the words of the Son of God. No other man ever spoke like He did. His words have outlasted any other words spoken by any other person.

Even though Jesus was only thirty years old when He began to speak, it is obvious that His words were not the words of a young zealot trying to impress people. They were the most profound sayings ever known to man.

Down through the centuries, men from all walks of life have commented on the uniqueness of the words of Jesus. I have produced a few of these quotations for your benefit.

[1] Jesus Christ is the outstanding personality of all time... no other teacher - Jewish, Christian, Buddhist, Mohammedan - is still a teacher whose teaching is such a guidepost for the world we live in. Other teachers may have something basic for an oriental, Arab, or an Occidental; but every act and word of Jesus has value for all of us. He became the light of the world. Why shouldn't I, a Jew be proud of that?

Sholem Ash

For when we consider what a large number of sayings are recorded of - or at least attributed to - Him, it becomes most remarkable that in literal truth there is no reason why any of his word should ever pass away in the sense of becoming obsolete...contrast Jesus Christ with other thinkers of like antiquity. Even Plato, who though some four hundred years before Christ in point in time, was greatly in advance of him in respect of philosophic thought, is nowhere in this respect as compared with Christ. Read the *Dialogues* and see how enormous is the contrast with the gospels in respect of errors of all kinds, reaching even into absurdity in respect of reason, and to sayings; shocking to the moral sense, yet this is confessedly the highest level of human reason on the lines of spirituality when unaided by alleged revelation.

G.J. Romanes

After reading the doctrines of Plato, Socrates or Aristotle, we feel the specific difference between their words and Christ's is the difference between an enquiry and a revelation.

Joseph Parker

For two thousand years, He [Jesus] *has* been the Light of the World and His words have *not* passed away.

Morris

His [Jesus] words were so completely parts and utterances of himself, that they had no meaning as abstract statements of truth uttered by him as a divine oracle of prophet. Take away himself as the primary (though not the ultimate) subject to every statement and they all fall to pieces.

F.J.A. Hort

But Jesus' words and acts are impressively integral and we trust those sayings we judge to be authentically his as revelatory of his person. When Jesus uses the personal pronoun 'I' ('but I say to you amen, I say to you') he stands and backs every word with personal fidelity and personal intentionality. If his words and acts are messianic in character, *it is because he intends them to be*, and if he intends them to be, then he is thinking of himself in messianic terms.

Gruenler

Christ's words are of permanent value because of his person; they endure because he endures.

Thomas

Statistically speaking, the gospels are the greatest literature ever written. They are read by more people, quoted by more authors, translated into more tongues, represented in more art, set to more music, than any other book or books written by any man in any century in any land.

But the words of Christ are not great based on the grounds that they have such a statistical edge over any others words. They are read more, quoted more, believed more and translated more because they are the greatest words ever spoken. And where is their greatness? Their greatness lies in their pure, lucid spirituality in dealing clearly, definitively, and authoritatively with the great problems that throb in the human breast; namely who is God? Does He love me? What should I do to please him? How does He look at my sin? How can I be forgiven? Where will I go when I die? How must I treat others?

No other man's words have the appeal of Jesus' words because no other man can answer those fundamental human questions as Jesus answered them. They are the kind of words and answers we would expect God to give, and we who believe in Jesus' deity have no problem as to why these words came from his mouth.

Bernard Ramm

Never did the speaker seek to stand more utterly alone than when He uttered His majestic utterance. Never did it seem more improbable that it should be fulfilled. But as we look across the centuries we see how it has been realized. His words have passed into law, they have passed into doctrines, they have passed into proverbs, they have passed into consolations, but they have never 'passed away'. What human teacher ever dared to claim an eternity for his words?

Maclean

Systems of human wisdom will come and go, kingdoms and empires will rise and fall, but for all time to come Christ will remain 'the Way, the Truth, and the Life'

Schaff

No revolution that has ever taken place in society can be compared to that which has been produced by the words of Jesus.

Mark Hopkins

Christ's message is inexhaustible. Each generation finds it new and exciting.

Thomas

It is something said, "Everything that Jesus said has been said before him by others". Let us grant that this is true, what then? Originality may or may not be a merit. If the truth has already been uttered, the merit lies in repeating it, and giving it new and fuller application. But there are other considerations to be borne in mind. We have no other teacher who so completely eliminated the trivial, the temporal, and the false from his system. No one selected just the eternal and the universal, and combined them in a teaching, where all these great truths found their congenial home. These parallels from the teachings of others to that of Christ are brought together from this quarter and from that; how is it that none of these teachers furnishes us with any parallel to the teachings of Christ? As a whole, while each of them gives us such truths as he expresses mingled with a mass of what is trivial and absurd? How was it that a carpenter, of no special training, ignorant of the culture and learning of the Greeks, born of a people whose great teachers were narrow, sour, intolerant pedantic legalists, was the supreme religious teacher the world has known, whose supremacy here makes him the most important figure in the world's history?

W.S. Peake

Though without formal rabbinical training, he showed no timidity of self-consciousness, no hesitation as to what he felt to be truth. Without any thought of himself or his audience, he spoke out fearlessly on every occasion, utterly heedless of the consequences to himself, and only concerned for truth and the delivery of his father's message. The power of his teaching was also deeply felt. "His word was with power" (Luke 4:32). The spiritual force of his personality expressed itself in his utterances and held his hearers in its enthralling grasp. And so we are not surprised to read of the impression of uniqueness made by him.(,) "never man spake like him" (John 7:46).

The simplicity and charm and yet the depth, the directness, the universality, and the truth of his teachings made a deep mark on his hearers, and elicited the conviction that they were in the presence of a teacher such as man had never seen before. And thus the proportion of teaching of the Gospel, and the impressions evidently created by the Teacher Himself, are such that we are not at all surprised that years afterwards the great Apostle of the Gentiles and His immediate followers, and in any full consideration of his person as the substance of Christianity great attention must necessarily be paid to his teaching.[1]

Griffith Thomas

If God became a man we would expect a superman with super sayings. These super sayings are what have been captured in red letters in some Bibles.

Characteristics of the Words of Jesus

1. **The sayings of Jesus were often so absolute that many have found them difficult to believe.**

Many of the words of Jesus appear to be extreme and are therefore ignored by a large number of believers.

But I say unto you, That whosoever is angry with his brother without a cause shall be in danger of the judgment: and whosoever shall say to his brother, Raca, shall be in danger of the council: but whosoever shall say, THOU FOOL, SHALL BE IN DANGER OF HELL FIRE.

Matthew 5:22

2.   The words of Jesus were not influenced by men.

Most speakers are influenced by their audience.   Ex-presidents give speeches and are paid over a hundred thousand dollars per session.   Obviously you would want to say things that impress and please your audiences.   Not so with Jesus. He had no one to please except His father. Jesus did not even attempt to get the respect of men.

I receive not honour from men.

John 5:41

It seemed He did not crave the approval of men; neither did He crave a large following. What He seemed to desire was to please His Father.

3.   The words of Jesus were so simple that they are rarely forgotten, even by children.

Once you hear either the sayings or the parables of Jesus, you rarely forget them. There have been many backslidden people who came back to God because they remembered their Sunday school Bible stories and Bible verses.

4.   The words of Jesus were easily understood by common people.

... And the common people heard him gladly.

Mark 12:37

5.   The words of Jesus were so anointed that they changed the lives of those that heard them.

It is the spirit that quickeneth; the flesh profiteth nothing: THE WORDS THAT I SPEAK UNTO YOU, THEY ARE SPIRIT, AND THEY ARE LIFE.

John 6:63

6.   The words of Jesus contain great love and kindness

Then came Peter to him, and said, Lord, how oft shall my brother sin against me, and I forgive him? till seven times? Jesus saith unto him, I say not unto thee, Until seven times: but, Until seventy times seven.

Matthew 18:21-22

7.   The words of Jesus are superior to the words of Peter, James, John and Paul.

Paul, Peter, James and John were the servants of Christ. Although the words of Jesus are lumped together with the teachings of Paul and other prophets, they should be separated because they are truly the words of God. It is only fitting that they be typed out in red. What Jesus said must be taken more seriously than what Paul or Peter said.

Remember that Paul is not the second son of God. Paul was a servant of Jesus Christ. The Lord has used the writings of Paul to bless the church but these cannot substitute the words of the Son of God himself. All that Paul, Peter or James taught must be received in this context. They were apostles building on the foundation laid by Christ Jesus.

The very fact that the Lord allowed other apostles to write should not become a snare to us. We must receive the writings of the other apostles but we must know the difference.

Christ set the greatest example of teamwork and fruitfulness. He did not prevent others from ministering. He encouraged them and did not mind if people were greatly blessed by these apostles. However it is up to us not to fall or walk into deception, but to recognize the words of Jesus as the ultimate and final statements of truth. The words of Jesus must be the guiding post for all Christians and ministers. We, must assess our ministries by the words of Jesus.

8. The words of Jesus define the standards of Heaven.

Our depraved and corrupt world has its own fallen standards for everything. Our estimation of good and bad is often very different from the standards of Heaven. We are often surprised to see what Jesus called the *greatest* or the *least*. Our human opinion is often a far cry from the judgment of God.

At the same time came the disciples unto Jesus, saying, WHO IS THE GREATEST in the kingdom of heaven? Whosoever therefore shall humble himself as THIS LITTLE CHILD, the same is greatest in the kingdom of heaven.

Matthew 18:1, 4

9. The words of Jesus contain the marking scheme for our final judgment.

And then will I profess unto them, I never knew you: depart from me, ye that work iniquity.

Matthew 7:23

What will we be judged about? What questions will we be asked on that great Day of Judgment? Jesus clearly outlined the basis for each one of our judgments. I know of no one who spoke with such clarity about life after death.

I have studied anatomy, physiology, biochemistry, pharmacology, chemical pathology etc. None of these books even broach the subject of what will happen after death. None of these books commented on this terrifying question. The research of all scientists ends at the grave.

The physicians arrive at a frontier they cannot cross. The philosophers reach the limits of their knowledge. The pathologist dissects the remains of the dead but cannot find out where the soul went. The professors stumble at the pertinent question of life after death. But not Jesus! He confidently describes the after-life with authority never seen before.

10. The words of Jesus contain the mysteries of Heaven.

These mysteries are reserved for those who would search and discover great truths for themselves.

It is the glory of God to conceal a thing: but the honour of kings is to search out a matter.

Proverbs 25:2

Furthermore, by these few pages, my son, be admonished because of making many books there is no end

Chapter 4

What Jesus Said about Glorifying God

HEREIN IS MY FATHER GLORIFIED, that ye bear much fruit; so shall ye be my disciples.

John 15:8

Jesus clearly shows us how the Father is glorified. God is glorified through the fruit we bear. The more fruit we bear, the more we bring glory to the father.

Independent or Fruitful?

Sometimes, you wonder what people are after. It is time to take the words of Jesus seriously. Some pastors are not content with bearing much fruit because they bear this fruit under the banner of another man's ministry.

I have watched as ministers have left the place of fruitfulness and moved into the deserts of ministry. *Perhaps, it is more important to them to be independent than to bear fruit.*

It should be the desire of every minister to bear much fruit. Unfortunately the desire for money, position and fame is not compatible with the desire for fruitfulness.

Fruitfulness must be on top of the agenda of every true man of God. Always ask yourself; what can I do to bear more fruit than I am already bearing. This is the reason why I want to have more churches. This is the reason I constantly press for church growth. That is why I write more books and preach as much as I do. I am striving for fruitfulness. I know that "Herein is the Father glorified…"

God placed the desire for fruitfulness in my heart. I have prayed for years that I would be fruitful.

For a brief period, I lived in Cleadon Village, Sunderland, England. Often, I was home alone and had a lot of time to pray. I always remember one rainy night when I walked up and down the road praying for fruitfulness. There are times you particularly remember your prayers because in that moment, you connected to heaven in a special way.

That night, I believe I connected to Heaven in a special way. I had one cry on my heart, "Lord make me fruitful." I was only twenty years old then but God heard my prayer and now, more than twenty years later, I see much fruit around me. But it is still not enough, I want to bring more glory to the Father by bearing even more fruit.

Unfortunately we have replaced God's explanation of what glorifies Him with our definition of what glorifies Him.

One day a brother came from the university campus with "good news". He said, "God is being glorified on campus, the Spirit is moving."

I was very interested to know what was happening so I asked, "Really, what is happening?"

With a broad smile he answered, "Many students have passed their exams!"

My brother had equated the passing of exams to the move of the Spirit of God. I explained to him that the passing of exams was a great thing but the indicator of the move of God was when people were saved and gifts of the Spirit manifested.

When our desires are met, we think God is being glorified. The hymn is sung "'To God be the glory great things He has done". To us, a new car or a new house means God is glorified.

When weddings take place we like to sing to the glory of God. The parents of the bride and groom will say, "God has glorified Himself today". The bride will say, "God has brought glory to His name."

Dear sister, I am sure there was glory at your wedding. But Jesus said He would be glorified when you bear much fruit.

Herein is my Father glorified, THAT YE BEAR MUCH FRUIT; so shall ye be my disciples.

John 15:8

Furthermore, by these few pages, my son, be admonished because of making many books there is no end

Chapter 5

Jesus' Method for Bringing Forth Much Fruit

I am the vine, ye are the branches: He that ABIDETH IN ME, and I IN HIM, the same bringeth forth much fruit: for without me ye can do nothing.

John 15:5

Staying connected to Jesus is the master key to bearing much fruit. Human effort can never substitute the effect of being deeply connected to Jesus. The fruit you bear is a result of your connection to God. Without walking in the ways and words of Jesus, you cannot bear fruit.

Without the connection to Jesus and the Father, there will be little fruit. The fruit of a man of God's ministry is therefore *a sign of his connection to the vine.*

A study of the vineyards of Palestine shows that some of the vines did not bear much fruit. They were vines alright but the connection to the roots was not deep and therefore they did not bear fruit. The fruit you bear is a reflection of the connection between you, the Father and Jesus.

By inference we could say that people who have no fruit are not connected to Him. Without Him you can do nothing. Everybody knows that! That means that people who are doing nothing are probably without Him.

Furthermore, by these few pages, my son, be admonished because of making many books there is no end

Chapter 6

What Jesus Said about Achievement

...for without me ye can do nothing.

John 15:5b

When Jesus was saying that without me you can do nothing, He was saying that without being spiritual, you cannot succeed in this life and you can do nothing. It may seem like some people achieve a lot without Him, but it is not so. "Except the Lord build the house, they labour in vain that build it" (Psalm 127:1).

Compare the Men of Babel with Abraham

Comparing the men of Babel gives tremendous insight to the concept of achievement. The men of Babel desired a great name but it was Abraham who got the great name. The men of Babel wanted to get to heaven but it was Abraham who got to heaven. It seems that a portion of heaven is even named after him - Abraham's bosom.

The story of the tower of Babel is a good example of men coming together to achieve something for themselves. They said let us build something for ourselves. Let us make a name for ourselves. Let us prevent ourselves from being scattered. God was not in their thoughts. They depended on the power of unity rather than on the power of God.

And they said, Go to, let us build us a city and a tower, whose top may reach unto heaven; and let us make us A NAME, lest we be scattered abroad upon the face of the whole earth.

Genesis 11:4

But without God, all their human efforts ended in confusion and fragmentation. Similarly all the efforts we make without God will end in confusion and scattering.

Many attempts to be happily married have ended in confusion and scattering. Divorce is the separation of families. Many attempts to be rich have ended in confusion. Many attempts at higher education and higher achievement have not brought the happiness men expected. The result has often been confusion and despair.

Who can do these things for us? Only the Lord can. Jesus said that we could do *nothing* without him.

Just a few verses after the unfortunate story of the men of Babel is the story of Abraham. Abraham lived a life of obedience to God. He did not try to achieve anything for himself. God told him, I will make you a great nation and I will bless you and make your name great.

And I will make of thee a great nation, and I will bless thee, and make thy name great; and thou shalt be a blessing:

Genesis 12:2

Isn't it amazing that all the goals of the men of Babel were given freely to Abraham? Abraham accomplished all the goals of the men of Babel. His achievements were only because he trusted God. Today, Abraham's name is great. Everyone in the world has heard of Abraham, including those in the most remote corners of Ghana.

Six thousand years later, Abraham has a great nation in Israel and the men of Babel have nothing! We all know that Abraham is in heaven because of the story of Lazarus and the Rich Man.

What a mighty God we serve. He is able to accomplish more than we can think or imagine. A life lived in obedience and faith towards God cannot be compared to a life of strenuous human efforts for self establishment.

That is why I am in the ministry, I am serving the Lord, I am obeying Him and I am living for Him. All I have is what He gives me. All I do is what I do with Him. Without Him I do not even want to live.

Furthermore, by these few pages, my son, be admonished because of making many books there is no end

29

Chapter 7

What Jesus Said about Decline

If a man abide not in me, he is cast forth as a branch, AND IS WITHERED; and men gather them, and cast them into the fire, and they are burned.

John 15:6

Jesus told us that when we do not abide in him He will cast us off and we will wither. 'To wither' means "to decline, to shrink," and "to be lowered in rank." In your life and ministry you must look out for these trends.

"To wither" also means "to decrease, to be lowered in rank" and "to be downgraded."

Sometimes a weakening and declining ministry is a result of disconnection from Jesus. Once the branch is disconnected from the vine, the withering begins. It is your duty to press close to the vine.

Stay connected to God! Press hard to stay close and to be intimate with God. God is always doing a new thing. Perhaps the Lord moved on long ago and you have been left behind. This may be the explanation for the decline and the downgrading of your ministry.

I once saw an amazing picture. It was the picture of a bridge over dry ground. Believe it or not the river had moved from under the bridge. This river had moved to the side of the bridge. Because of this, the bridge no longer passed over water but over dry land. This had happened because of a severe flood. After the floodwaters dropped, the river had amazingly shifted! "What would they do now that the river has shifted?" Would they still use the old bridge? I have outlined below a few of the possibilities.

1.   You could say that we invested a lot of money in this bridge and therefore we are not going to abandon it now.

2.   You could say, "This bridge has worked for us from the beginning and we don't see why it will not work now".

3.   "We have sentimental and emotional feelings for this bridge and cannot bring ourselves to abandoning it".

4.   You could also say, "This is the way we've done it all these years and we are going to be faithful to our original bridge".

5.   "We don't have enough money to build a new one."

6.   I am sure some would say, "It will take too much to start something new."

Dear pastor, wake up to the realities. Things have changed! If you do not accept the fact that the river has moved and decide to build a new bridge, the usefulness of your bridge will decline. There will be no one walking on your bridge anymore.

Your ministry is like that bridge. Many souls walked on it onto salvation because then, it was relevant. Your bridge is connected to the right spots on the ground.   But when your bridge is no longer connected to the right spot, people will not need it anymore. The number of people who cross the bridge will decline.

Oh, how many ministries and Men of God wither because of this? Often it is not the presence of sin, but they are not connected, abiding in Christ. They are not learning the new things that God is doing. They are disconnected from the current move of God.

Furthermore, by these few pages, my son, be admonished because of making many books there is no end

Chapter 8

How Jesus Will Decide Who the Greatest Is

Whosoever therefore shall humble himself as this little child, THE SAME IS GREATEST in the kingdom of heaven.

Matthew 18:4

I once attended an international gathering of pastors of large churches. These were pastors of the largest churches in their countries. All the pastors had an air of importance around them. Most of us were preoccupied with ourselves and how successful we had been in our respective nations. I wondered to myself; who is the most successful pastor here? Who is the greatest?

I sat by one American pastor who asked me about the income of my church. I hesitated. He then told me the income of his church. I did a quick calculation in my head and I realized that this pastor takes in one month what I take in a year. I became even more hesitant to declare the income of my church. It sounded too little to be true.

Then another American mentioned how much he spent on television per hour. I realized that he paid for one hour what I paid for one year of TV broadcast. As we moved around the room chatting and making friends I would ask: "what is your church like?"

One person would mention; "I have sixteen thousand members", "I have twenty thousand members", "I have eleven thousand members". I tell you, I couldn't find anybody with less than ten thousand members! I became intimidated as I walked among the 'greats' in ministry.

Later on, I met these pastors at the Hilton Hotel of that city. Many of them were at ease in the environment of wealth. They had traveled first class and were very comfortable in a five star environment. Of course I was also happy to be there and made myself comfortable.

Later that night, I thanked God for putting me amongst the greatest pastors on earth. Surely, I thought, I must now be one of the greatest pastors too.

"This is the company I want to be in", I mused. "And I am going to stay close to these wonderful and great men of God".

Later on, we attended the conference and when I arrived in the entrance lobby, the administrator walked up to me and stuck a badge with some little flowers on me. I looked at it and it said "V.I.P".

I thought to myself; "I am going higher with every passing minute." I looked around to see whether other people had this same badge and I noticed that it was just a select few who had this badge. Those of us with the V.I.P. badges were escorted to the front rows of the hall. As I sat on the front row, I looked back and knew God had lifted me from the ranks and had promoted me.

When I was finally leaving the conference, I was taken to the airport in a fantastic black, executive car. I felt like a president. Finally I knew that God had elevated me in the ministry. As I sat in the back of my car, I noticed all kinds of modern gadgets including a television. I pressed a few of the buttons and enjoyed the fancy gadgets in the car. I sat back, crossed my legs and enjoyed the ride to the airport. The car was like a large executive sitting room. Surely I had reached the heights of ministry and was rubbing shoulders with the greatest. I now had my confirmation that I was indeed one the greatest.

It was years later that the Lord gave me a new understanding of who He considered to be great. The greatest amongst us is the most humble. Jesus never talked about the size of your church, the car you drive, or the money you have. *The divine measurement of greatness is completely different from the earthly.*

Actually, the greatest pastor at that conference was the most humble amongst us. Unfortunately success and wealth are usually not bedfellows of humility. Most wealthy and successful people lose the humility they had. The greatest amongst us was not the one with the V.I.P. badge, but the most humble one at heart. Thank God that it is possible to be humanly great and also great in the eyes of God. We must strive for greatness in the sight of God.

One day I sat with a group of my pastors. I told them, you may be greater than me in heaven. They laughed. "How could you say something like that?" They were so used to submitting to me and seeing me ahead of them.

I asked them "can you not imagine me serving you in heaven?"

I told them; "don't be deceived by what you see on earth. The greatest amongst us is the most humble at heart". The first shall be last and the last shall be first.

Mercy Lord! *Zee**!

Furthermore, by these few pages, my son, be admonished because of making many books there is no end

*The Expression "Zee" is the author's colloquial exclamation.

Chapter 9

How Jesus Defined the Work of God

Jesus answered and said unto them, This is the work of God, THAT YE BELIEVE on him whom he hath sent.

John 6:29

Verily, verily, I say unto you, HE THAT BELIEVETH ON ME, the works that I do shall he do also; and greater works than these shall he do; because I go unto my Father.

John 14:12

I have always used John 14:12 as a standard for my life, a mark I must attain. To be able to do the works of Jesus and possibly, greater works, is one of my goals. Most of the time, I forget about the greater works. At least, I want to be able to do the works that Jesus did. Jesus' works were preaching, teaching and healing.

These Scriptures above explain why we do not see the works of Jesus in many churches. The only condition for doing these great works is believing. He did not say that any one who was anointed would do the greater works. He did not say anyone who had seen a vision would do the greater works. He said, "he that believeth, the works that I do shall he do also and greater works than these shall he do.

The Key

John 6:29 gives a direct key to doing the works of Jesus. Many times, I have asked myself how I can do these works of God? But it is a question that Jesus answered.

The simple answer from Jesus was *"believe"*. Of course we all claim to believe but why are we not able to do these great works?

I know that we would have expected Jesus to say something like pray more, be holy, seek the face of God; but all He said was "believe".

A little analysis will reveal that most of us do not really believe the words of Jesus. Let me give you two scriptures that we commonly disbelieve. I say that we do not believe because our lives demonstrate *the exact opposite* of these scriptures.

1.   I go to prepare a place for you

In my Father's house are many mansions: if it were not so, I would have told you. I go to prepare a place for you.

John 14:2

If we believed that the Lord was preparing a place for us, our lives would be quite different. However, by the attitude of the ordinary Christians, it is obvious that we have little regard for these words of Jesus. If He is preparing a place for us, that is all well and good. But we need some mansions *here and now*. We couldn't care two hoots about any mansion in the sky. We need a mansion in town and we want it now. This very attitude keeps us from being eternally minded. Because Christians do not consider eternity, they are unable to really work for God.

2.   Don't lay up treasures on earth.

LAY NOT UP for yourselves TREASURES UPON EARTH...But lay up for yourselves treasures in heaven...

Matthew 6:19-20

There could be no clearer instruction than this. He said, "Prepare for heaven. Lay up your treasure over there. Do not bother to pile up things on earth".

Yet most of the church, led by its pastors, are busy laying up treasures on earth. Even when we are poor, we have a goal to lay up as much treasure on this earth. Our vision is to do the exact opposite of what Jesus asked us to do. As long as we do not picture treasures in heaven, we will be unmotivated to work for God.

The ordinary Christian is highly motivated to work for Barclays Bank or any other bank. They see it as a way to lay up treasures on earth. How difficult it is for us to leave prestigious secular jobs and work in the church. It is seen as the highest kind of folly. To work in the church is perceived as madness. Working for God makes you lay up treasures in heaven.

A professor of the Medical School once asked his staff, "where do you go to church?"

When the professor found out that he came to my church, he laughed for several minutes. Then he asked, "This Dag Heward-Mills, is he normal?"

"Why do you ask whether he is normal?" asked the gentleman.

The professor answered, "Does a normal person behave that way? Does a normal medical student start a church in a classroom?" Then he continued laughing.

One lady was told that she needed to see a psychiatrist because she wanted to work in the ministry instead of elsewhere. These anti-work-for-God attitudes are also attitudes of born-again Christians. It was a born-again Christian who thought his sister ought to see a psychiatrist for wanting to work in the church.

Such disbelief is not found only amongst unbelieving professors but also amongst born-again charismatic believers. This attitude which despises eternal work is found in my own church. It is found amongst lay pastors. It is even found amongst full-time pastors who pray that their children will never work for a church.

Laying up treasures in Heaven is a truth we choose to ignore. Laying up treasures on earth (the exact opposite of what Jesus taught) is seen as the more sensible thing to do.

It is these amazing attitudes that show what we really believe. It is no wonder that we cannot do much of the work of God. Moslems often show a much higher faith in the life after this life. Their suicide-bombers are the greatest evidence of this. All over the world, these suicide-bombers die fearlessly for their faith. Meanwhile, Christians cower in fear, disbelief and weakness, unable even to change jobs for the gospel's sake. *Merzee**!

Where are the missionaries of old who gave their lives in foreign nations that the gospel may advance? Where are the martyrs of the early church who died for their faith? These heavenly-minded people laid down their lives for the kingdom of God to advance. These men, conscious of eternity have brought real advancement to the church of God.

They really demonstrated that they believed and that is how come they did the works of God.

*The expression "merzee" is the author's colloquial exclamation.

Chapter 10

What Jesus Said about Sacrifice

And when he had called the people unto him with his disciples also, he said unto them, Whosoever will come after me, let him deny himself, AND TAKE UP HIS CROSS, and FOLLOW ME.

Mark 8:34

Take up Your Cross

Jesus said we should take up our cross and follow him. This speaks of sacrifice. Oh, how we sacrifice for other things. Our pastors and our churches are earthly-minded.

Don't you see that a new gospel that teaches us to grasp at earthly things has replaced the words of Jesus?

Thousands of people followed Jesus until he told then to drink his blood and eat his body. As soon as Jesus preached about sacrifice, his church reduced in size. But that is how to do the works of Jesus. To believe in the cross and all that it stands for.

I believe that the preaching of the cross will be become popular again. The preaching of the cross is the preaching of the true Gospel. It is time to return to the cross. It is time to sing about the cross again.

Today, Christians believe more in their earthly existence than their heavenly reward. If we were to pay the same price we pay for earthly things, perhaps the works of God would be done.

I once spoke to a doctor and asked how many years he had studied medicine for. He answered; "about twenty two years." I thought to myself, "is it not marvelous? Someone can spend twenty-two years of his life to acquire a profession he will use for another twenty years. But how many days of our lives in order to follow Jesus?"

Unfortunately, we don't really believe the ministry is something worth dying for.

I always ask myself, "What is the difference between my ministry and that is of Christ?" Where are the healings? Where is the preaching and the teaching?

If you want to follow Jesus you must believe in the reality of sacrifice. You must follow the example of Jesus and pay the high price God is asking of you. You must preach about the cross. *You* must take up your cross. You cannot sit in the bank and send people to the cross. It doesn't work that way. *You* have to take up *your* cross and follow Jesus who took up *His* cross!

Furthermore, by these few pages, my son, be admonished because of making many books there is no end

Chapter 11

The Key to New Dimensions in Ministry

And said, Verily I say unto you, Except ye be converted, and BECOME AS LITTLE CHILDREN, ye shall not ENTER into the kingdom of heaven.

Matthew 18:3

Pastors are often the opposite of children. They get to a point where they cannot be taught any longer. Most pastors do not listen to tapes. They do not say "Amen" when the preaching is going on. They do not lift up their hands when the worship is going on.

Most pastors would never respond to an altar call, no matter how much they needed the prayer. We are so conscious of ourselves and would not like to look foolish before anyone.

Because we are so different from children, we are unable to enter the Kingdom. Salvation is not the only thing that requires a childlike attitude. Childlikeness is required to enter every other department of the Kingdom of God.

You will not enter a higher dimension of preaching or church growth because you refuse to be childlike. A child is ready to learn something new. A child believes that he doesn't know everything. Children believe almost every fairy tale. But you believe almost nothing. *Merzee*!

I have had to be childlike to improve my preaching. I have constantly modified my style and approach to preaching. Initially my preaching was commonsensical because the person I understudied was a rational, common sense teacher. With time I realized that my people were more open to stirring, rousing and exciting preaching. I decided to learn how to do that as well. I had to learn this from those who were good at it.

I had to be childlike and open to a completely different kind of ministry. When you are a rational, common sense preacher it is easy to look down on inspirational, emotional and encouraging speakers. With pride, you disdain them because they don't seem to say much. There does not seem to be much substance in their many words. You think to yourself, "He does not have enough points or Scriptures."

Childlikeness in the ministry will enable you to learn from anyone including people below you and people you don't respect. You will never look down on another man of God and consider him to be irrelevant. You will know that there is something to learn from everyone.

I often learn something from every church I visit. Recently one of my branch churches had a special dress down outreach service and I thought it was an excellent idea. I decided to copy them immediately. I have no problem learning from my own sons in the ministry.

Most of us are kept out of new dimensions of ministry because of our pride and self-importance. How could I be superior to another minister? Why would I be overconfident and develop an air of self-importance? This attitude keeps us from entering newer and higher dimensions of ministry.

There was a time in my ministry; I didn't minister the Spirit much. However there was a pastor who flowed in all kinds of weird manifestations of the Spirit. I was curious, I was childlike, and I wanted to learn as much as I could. I began to attend programmes where he was ministering. I also invited him to our church. I would watch in amazement as this pastor ministered under a peculiar anointing. Every kind of manifestation of the Spirit would take place. I once saw a lady moving on the floor like a snake!

One day, this pastor was invited to another church and he ministered there for a few days. I later met the pastor who invited him. I was surprised at the derogatory remarks he made about this "minister of manifestations". He confidently intimated that , "These manifestations take us nowhere and there is nothing to them."

But I wondered to myself, "Why is this pastor cutting himself away from something new?" We often cut ourselves away from new and higher dimensions of God's Kingdom. No one knows it all. God has intentionally given bits of knowledge to different parts of His body. This is God's design. It is intended to humble us. It is intended to make us need each other and ask each other for help.

What can be more humbling than to have to ask someone for help? Because I had a childlike (learner's) attitude towards the manifestations of the Spirit, I now minister and flow comfortably in that area.

I remember when I wanted to go into the healing ministry. I prayed about it and asked the Lord what to do. The Lord pointed out a particular minister to me. He told me to follow him and I would receive the anointing to minister to the sick. As I began to listen to this minister's tapes, I found them difficult to understand.

My wife found them even more difficult to comprehend. Once, I said to myself, "What kind of preaching is this? No one could possibly understand it." But I kept on listening to his tapes and following his ministry. As I humbled myself and continued, a day came when things began to fall in place. I suddenly understood what was going on and could follow the message. I would watch him minister and I would get blessed. I began to know what to do in the healing ministry. Gradually, I climbed into a very difficult but worthwhile dimension of ministry. *What a humbling journey it is to enter into new dimensions of God's Kingdom!*

Dear pastor, you may be kept out of many wonderful aspects of God's Kingdom because you are not childlike. A child does not look at age, sex or background! A child simply receives! Humble yourself in the sight of the Lord and He will lift you into new dimensions of ministry!

Furthermore, by these few pages, my son, be admonished because of making many books there is no end

Chapter 12

The Motivation for Pastors

But I receive not testimony from man: but these things I say, that ye might be saved.

John 5:34

How can ye believe, which receive honour one of another, and seek not the honour that cometh from God only?

John 5:44

The "honour of man" is the single greatest influence on ministers apart from the Holy Spirit. The honour of man is simply the respect and admiration that comes from other men in society.

Jesus made it clear that He did not receive respect and admiration from men. This means that He did not do anything because men would honour Him. He explained, "How can you believe which receive honour one from another?" In other words how can you flow with God when it is important for you to have the respect and the honour of men?

I have discovered that the honour of men is the single most powerful determinant of what people do. Without knowing it, most of us have a group of human beings whose admiration and respect we crave. We long for them to approve of us and to admire our achievements. Our schooling, our spouses, our cars, houses, food, and our clothes are all designed to attract the credit of people around us. Just like the Holy Spirit, the honour of man is an invisible influence, but it is very real.

Virtually every decision a ministry makes is a decision between following the Holy Spirit and following the honour of men.

Let me give you seven examples:

1. The honour of man will prevent you from becoming a pastor.

When I became a pastor initially, there were not many pastors in town. It was not an honourable thing to become a pastor. I heard people ridiculing me for calling myself a pastor. The thoughts of people's impressions of me could have kept me from obeying the call of God.

2. The honour of man will prevent you from having a church.

Having a church in the part of the city where our church is, was also challenging. It is situated at Korle Gonno, one of the deprived and difficult parts of Accra, Ghana. Who would want to come to church in such an area? The church building that we had acquired sat in the middle of a huge rubbish dump. Were we building a church to receive the admiration of men or were we building under the influence of the Holy Spirit?

Many years ago when I became a Christian, I would not have joined the church I did if the honour and admiration of men had been important to me. The church I joined was started by a former drug addict who had not gone beyond class three in school. I once took my little sisters to that church and they could not contain their laughter for one and a half hours as they listened to amazing grammatical blunders. The church service was held in the corridor of the pastor's father's house. My elitist family and friends could not easily relate with such a church and such a pastor.

Was I looking for the respect and admiration of the elitist community of Accra? Or was I looking to find the glory of God? I receive not honour from men.

3.   The honour of man sometimes directs people to marry the wrong person.

Amazingly, we seem to need the approval and endorsement of people in our little world for even a marriage partner. There are people who marry doctors because the community will admire the marriage partnership. What do people say and what does God say? What people say seems to be so strong that it has virtually taken control of men of God. Don't forget what Jesus said: That which is highly esteemed in the sight of men is an abomination in the sight of God.

And he said unto them, Ye are they which justify yourselves before men; but God knoweth your hearts: for that which is HIGHLY ESTEEMED among men is ABOMINATION in the sight of God.

Luke 16:15

Unfortunately, the honour of men which is so powerful in its influence, leads us to choose things which are an abomination to the Lord. Could it be that you put aside the will of God because you did not have the admiration of men? Perhaps you married an abomination because you sought the honour of men. Perhaps, in seeking for the admiration of men, you left the godly option and chose the wrong person. I receive not honour from men!

4. The honour of man will stop you from preaching the messages that God wants you to preach.

I would have changed the message I preached if I were looking for the honour of men. There are dignified messages that appeal to the intellect of the upper class and aristocratic community of my city. I could impress them with high-sounding words and secular teachings.

Someone once said my preaching was too simple. I thought to myself, "Who was simpler than Christ? Even little children understand His teachings." There are times people have even wondered whether I speak English properly because I don't speak with a certain polished diction.

I want to be like Paul who said:

And I, brethren, when I came to you, came not with excellency of speech or of wisdom, declaring unto

**you the testimony of God. For I determir
know any thing among you, save Jesus C...
him crucified.**

1 Corinthians 2:1-2

I have stayed with the message of salvation and soul-winning. I know that I do not sound as impressive and dignified as some may want. But do I want to please God or do I want to please men? Paul said that if he pleased men, then he was not a servant of God.

For do I now persuade men, or God? or do I seek to please men? for if I yet pleased men, I should not be the servant of Christ.

Galatians 1:10

Notice that pleasing men actually conflicts with our service to God. Why would Paul say that if he pleased men then he could not be a servant of God? It is because pleasing men is often diametrically opposed to pleasing God.

When I began to show my miracles services on TV, some of my church members appealed that I show only teaching services. They told me how some university lecturers were very impressed with my teaching services, and were worried that I would lose the respect and admiration of such noble people.

"What will they think about you when they see you pouring oil on hundreds of people? What will they think when they see people falling down and screaming in the church service?" they asked me.

Did people fall down and scream when Jesus ministered to them?

And when the unclean spirit had torn him, and CRIED WITH A LOUD VOICE, he came out of him.

Mark 1:26

Do I want to be like Jesus or do I want to be what the professor in the university wants me to be?

Ministering to the sick is not possible when you love the honour of men. You will stay as far away as possible from that if you want the respect and admiration of the upper class of society. You see, the noble have surgeons and doctors ready to treat them in European and American hospitals. They don't seek solutions in the church. When people stand to testify that they are healed of headaches and pain in the knees, the noble chuckle in disdain.

One night, a medical doctor watched me minister to the sick on TV. He sent a message to me through a doctor who was a member of my church. He said, "Tell Dag that if he wants to heal the sick he should come right here to the ward. We have sarcomas, chondroblastomas, cancers of the knee, and many other wild diseases on the ward. Tell him this is where the action is. He should come here to perform his wonders." This fellow made other condescending remarks about the ministry.

Having worked on the ward before, I know what is there. I do know that spiritual healing looks ridiculous in the eyes of surgeons, physicians, paediatricians and obstetricians. The question is: "Do I care about looking foolish before such people? Do I care about being despised by my medical colleagues and fellow doctors? Whose respect and admiration do I want? Jesus Christ's or Professor Big Stuff's?" I receive not honour from men.

5. The honour of man will prevent you from being full-time in ministry.

Being full-time in ministry would be impossible if I wanted the respect and admiration of men. My own father told me he could not imagine his son eating off the collection of church members.

Let me ask you a question, "In the eyes of men, which is more honourable: living off the collections of the poor masses or living from the income of a surgeon? Which of these would win more admiration: Being a pastor of a church in a slum of Accra or being a gynaecologist in Manhattan?" I want to be like Jesus and I want to be able to say, "I receive not honour from men."

Perhaps, there are more gifted people with higher callings than myself. However, many of these callings were never fulfilled because men loved the admiration of other men. I receive not honour from men!

But all their works they do for to be seen of men...

Matthew 23:5

6. The honour of man will lead you to possess things you shouldn't possess.

Perhaps you fear the scorn and disapproval of men. I tell you that if there is any one thing that guides us, it is this disease I call "seeking the honour of men".

The cars that we drive are often dictated by the honour of men. We have to drive cars with particular names. We sacrifice so much in order to have certain types of cars so that human beings would admire and endorse us.

There was a time that I was afflicted by this disease. Without knowing it, I wanted to drive certain cars to make men respect me. I realized that I was looking for men's admiration. Without knowing it, I wanted them to be in awe of my wealth and power. Like many pastors do, I unconsciously thought people would respect my ministry because of my car.

As I grew up in the Lord, I didn't want people to notice me as I passed by, much less notice the car that I drove. I receive not honour from men!

7. The honour of man will stop you from raising the funds necessary for ministry work.

I once had a meeting with some pastors and told them about a need to take up some special offerings. I told them to lay aside their dignity and to seriously exhort the people to give. I explained to them, "If you guys do not receive the offering seriously, it will greatly affect the plans we have for the ministry."

Some weeks later, I found out that some of the pastors had ignored my instructions. So I met them again to find out why they had not taken the offerings the way I taught them. It was then that I realized that many of these pastors were under the influence of the honour of man.

Even though they were pastors, they were concerned about their reputation in the ministry. They did not want the congregation to think they were the kind who were into the ministry for money. They wanted to look good and dignified at all times. Because I am a full-time minister, I had already lost that dignified stance where I could distance myself from money issues.

Many times, without knowing it, the honour of man has been the strongest influence on ministers. Why wouldn't you want to stand on the corner of a street and preach? It is because you think you are a dignified pastor who is above the ranks of a zealous new convert. The church has shifted away from many practical things that yield tangible results. We don't care if the great commission is not fulfilled, once we can keep the good name we think we have in society.

Most pastors seem to want the approval and friendship of heads-of-state and government officials. Today friendship with presidents and politicians is used as a credential and stamp of approval. Have you noticed that Jesus never visited Herod or Pontius Pilate? He never sought to be friends with these secular authorities. How different we are today.

Pastors travel from nation to nation, meeting one president after another. When we tell our congregations that we met the President of *Milagabostal city*, for instance, there is a thundering applause of approval. However, if we inform them that 15 converts were won in *Potomanto village*, there is a deafening silence, as the congregation doesn't seem to understand what it means! Meanwhile, there is great rejoicing in Heaven over one soul that is saved. Which Bible verse says, "There is great rejoicing in Heaven over one president that is visited?" It seems we are not looking for the applause of Heaven but the applause of men.

But all their works they do for TO BE SEEN OF MEN...

Matthew 23:5

The big ministries which could reach the remote villages and towns of our nations rarely spend any time, effort or money on these places.

One day, I travelled to the north of Ghana for evangelism and church planting. I later discussed the trip with a pastor friend. When I mentioned that I had planted a church in that place, he sniggered and said, "You do well to plant churches in such places. As for me, I don't go to such places."

I thought about his schedule. I realized that even though his ministry could afford to reach remote areas, it hardly did so. Perhaps God had not called him to such harvest fields. On the other hand, it is possible that God had called him, but he found it easier to work where men would recognize and endorse his ministry.

Dear friend, it is easier to work in the cities where men can endorse your ministry. After all, no one sees you when you are in that village. Don't forget that the honour of God is far more important than the approval and honour of men. I receive not honour from men!

Furthermore, by these few pages, my son, be admonished because of making many books there is no end

Chapter 13

Jesus Rebukes the Pastors

And love the uppermost rooms at feasts, and the chief seats in the synagogues, And greetings in the markets, and to be called of men, Rabbi, Rabbi.

Matthew 23:6-7

Unfortunately, the church today has become very similar to the group of people Christ encountered when He ministered on earth. Pastors today have developed similar characteristics to Pharisees and Sadducees.

I never knew that where a pastor sat was so important. My first encounter with this phenomenon was when a great healing evangelist visited Ghana. I noticed the politics that surrounded "who sits where". It was very important for people to be seated in front and on stage.

I myself really wanted to be on stage, where the action was. I witnessed a regrettable incident, in which a very senior pastor had taken his seat in the front row. Suddenly, the host pastor and one of the healing evangelist's associates came up and pointed to him and said, "You, move." This senior minister was shocked as he was moved to the second row, to sit by me. I felt very sad about this.

On another occasion, a great man of God visited us in Ghana. This was another huge event where thousands were in attendance. We had invited all the great pastors of our nation to be at the programme. No matter how I tried, it seemed I would offend somebody. One of the pastors was deeply offended that I would put him on the second row whilst others he felt were junior to him were on the first row. Because of this, he shunned the rest of the programme.

Nowadays, whenever I have such programmes, I am always scared that I will offend somebody. I try my best to treat everyone with the greatest dignity and respect. But there always seems to be some problem.

Can you believe that my greatest headache when organizing a crusade is not the counselling of the new converts but the seating arrangement of the bigwig pastors?

One day, whilst discussing how to organize another big event, I said to my fellow organizer, "I have a bright idea, why don't we have a stage without any seats so that everyone sits in the congregation?" We tried to implement this plan but it just wouldn't work. We ended up overcrowding our stage with so many chairs so that no one would be offended! Even then, our struggle wasn't over. Who was going to sit on the first row?

Dear friend, what is important is not where we sit. The greatest in Heaven is the servant and not the most impressive pastor.

But he that is greatest among you shall be your servant. And whosoever shall exalt himself shall be abased; and he that shall humble himself shall be exalted.

Matthew 23:11-12

Once, I met with a group of young men and ladies who wanted to be pastors. I asked them, "Why do you want to be pastors?" None of them gave a satisfactory answer. It seemed they just wanted to be appointed as pastors. So I asked them, "Have you become like the Pharisees? You love greetings in the public places. You love to be called "pastor, pastor".

Instead of loving God and loving His people, we love the acclamation which comes with the ministry. Mercy forever! I do not write this because I am any different. I am as guilty as any one else. May God help us all!

Ministers are unknowingly prey to pride, insecurity, and the fear of man. Without knowing it, our greatest influence is not the Holy Spirit. Other spirits like the fear of man have become our guiding posts. The following vision illustrates the point I am trying to make.

A Vision of Music Ministers Intermingling with Snakes

[2]This is the vision: I was standing in a well-known hotel lobby, which I had literally stood in earlier that same day during a very well-known Christian music conference. In the vision the very large and open lobby was packed full, as it usually is, with men and women from all over. Many were artists, musicians or people

directly involved in the business of music. The people were busy talking and going on with their business (what is commonly called 'schmoozing'), each one dressed up in appropriate music attire.

Much to my astonishment and horror, I saw what looked like a massive snake lying on the lobby floor. I could not even begin to calculate its length, but it easily covered the full length of the room. Its fat middle was at least six feet in height and looked almost twenty feet in width. It looked totally stuffed. Amazingly, people were actually leaning up against it!

I could hardly believe what I was seeing. My first impulse was to yell and warn everyone, but I hesitated because no one else seemed to notice it--they just carried on with their business. Many people were surrounded, and some were even totally wrapped up in its monstrous coils, and yet they were still unaware. They all were in great danger. I couldn't tell if the people could not see what I was seeing, or if they had simply grown accustomed to this monster. It almost seemed welcome here.

I wondered, "Who let this thing in here? Surely the thing has to be dead for people to be standing this close to it and still be this comfortable with it."

Then it happened...IT MOVED. I couldn't believe that something that looked so heavy could actually move. But it did. It slowly poured itself in between a few groups of preoccupied people so as not to disturb anyone. It was silent, and no one saw it move. No one seemed to have a sense of danger. This was extremely confusing to me. It looked like many in this place, for some reason, had totally dropped their guard. Obviously, this seemed crazy because of what I was seeing. As I stood there, greatly perplexed by this strange scenario, I was suddenly struck with the terrifying sense that there were other snakes in the room.

I reluctantly and cautiously gazed across the room. We were surrounded! The oversized serpents were everywhere! As I continued to observe the situation, my emotions began to evolve rapidly from initial shock and terror into great frustration because no one else seemed to be aware of these snakes. Soon I was filled with a sense of compassion for the blinded victims, and finally an intense anger gripped me because these creatures had somehow infiltrated this place.

That was it. That was all I saw at first. But I knew immediately that the great snakes I had seen in this vision were the principalities and dark powers (or evil spirits) that have been controlling and manipulating much of Christian music (ministry). I knew I had seen exactly what the small group of us had just been praying about, and I told them what I had seen. It was as if a small movie screen had appeared before me and shown me these things, even color.

The vision stayed with me for about 24 hours. I was surprised that it did. I guess I had hoped that what I had seen at first was the end of it, for it was not pleasant to dwell on. But it remained very graphic and the images would not go away. After starting to get literally sick to my stomach over what I had seen, my curiosity began to grow and I began wondering what the meaning of it was. Believing there had to be a reason for this lingering scene, I finally began to ask the Lord to show me the full meaning of the vision.

He did, and this is what was revealed next:[2]

Ministers and the Demon of Self-Promotion

[2]I was taken back to the same lobby and was shown each snake in vivid detail.

The first snake that was revealed to me was the first one that I had seen earlier, it was definitely the biggest one, easily filling the full length of the large lobby with its great coils wrapped around everywhere. This grayish colored snake was so large that it took me quite some time to find its huge head. I finally spotted the head hiding in the twisted masses of the mammoth coils. It had a hollow and yet all-consuming look upon its face. One word came into my mind as I studied its massive head--HUNGER. I then observed that it had just finished devouring something, or someone. I instinctively knew it was the latter. This snake was actually feeding on the people in the lobby and still no one seemed to notice!

This serpent had the ability to slowly surround its victims with enormous coils and then swallow them whole without them even being aware of it. I knew by its immense size and its lumpy and very bloated body that it had swallowed many victims. And much to my surprise, I could see the victims were still alive inside of it. They were moving inside the creature's ever-stretched belly. I could hear them still carrying on ambitious conversations with others in the lobby.

The serpent's name was **"Self-Promotion."**

Most of the victims did not know they had been consumed by self-promotion. But some, much to my dismay, had willingly and consciously allowed the snake to engulf them. The goal or intentions of these victims was the same as that of this bloated serpent--they all wanted to become bigger and BIGGER.[2]

Ministers and the Demons of Pride and Insecurity

[2]The next snake I saw, were two very long snakes. They were intertwined --wrapped all around each other just like snakes do when they are mating. This, by the way is exactly what these were doing. One was red; the other was yellow. They were spinning over and over, making a very uneasy sound that pervaded the whole place. As they twisted and spun around, they appeared to be actually biting each other. All at once I understood that this writhing mass was **"Pride"** and **"Insecurity"**. They were feeding off each other, and they were reproducing after their own kind.

Then I looked around the room and saw people who were turning yellow and then red. Yellow was the color of Insecurity and red was the color of pride. People would change these shades back and forth just like the rotating colors of the spinning serpents.

The whole lobby seemed aglow with these colors. The two worked well together, though they seemed to irritate one another.

There was a nervous uneasiness building that made me want to scream. These two serpents made those who were affected by them (which were almost everyone, to some extent) feel miserable. However, they didn't want to admit it, because their pride told them that they might look weak, insecure or possibly unsuccessful. So the spinning continued. Pride, Insecurity, Pride, Insecurity etc.[2]

Ministers and the Demon of the Fear of Man

[2]I was surprised that I even detected what was next. I knew it was only because the Lord was allowing me to see it--I never would have noticed it on my own. I spotted what had first appeared to be someone who had fallen down, but that it was much too long to be human. It was hidden half way under the front counter and was entangled among the feet of the people.

The reason I had originally believed it was human was because it appeared to have human skin or flesh. It had what looked like a human head. Though having the color of flesh and having no scales, it was obviously still a snake. It was very low to the ground and earthly.

This one was the **"the Fear of Man"**. It didn't have to do very much, because Pride and Insecurity were doing most of its work. It just lay there moving its human-like head back and forth horizontally. Then I noticed that people all across the room were doing the very same thing, almost as if they had been entranced They were only concerned about who was who, and they did not recognize the evil in their midst. This freaky creature blinded its victims from the holy fear of God and injected them with a deadly fear of man instead.

People all across the room were so busy looking at each other that they were unaware that they had become entangled by the fear of man. It would subtly wrap itself around its victims' feet until they could no longer move; they were completely paralyzed with fear. I remember the scripture: the fear of man will prove to be a snare (Proverbs 29:25).[2]

Ministers and the Demon of Jealousy

[2]I then heard a movement above me. I instinctively looked up, and there, much to my distress, I saw another serpent wrapped around the balcony, its endless tail running down the length of the escalator. This one was bright green. It looked like one of those tree snakes --very comfortable with heights. This was **"Jealousy"** and it was literally green with envy. It was breathing very heavily and seemed to have fire in its eyes. I could tell it was burning up inside. I didn't want it to catch me looking at it, because I was afraid it was ready to explode with fury at any moment.

Jealousy attacked the high places; it couldn't stand to be down low. Its mist-like breath released a fog of competition which filled the room, I could see that those who had breathed in the mist although they were chatting politely with peers, now had that same fire burning down in their eyes as did the serpent. And I knew they would attack and tear down those in the high places in order to obtain these places for themselves. Many of these people had become easy prey for Self-Promotion. [2]

Furthermore, by these few pages, my son, be admonished because of making many books there is no end

Chapter 14

The Priorities of Jesus

The priorities of Jesus are revealed in the Gospels. Whenever Jesus used the word "FIRST", He was teaching us that there were some things that had priority over others. You will notice from the Scriptures below how Jesus commanded us to do certain things first (before others).

> **Therefore if thou bring thy gift to the altar, and there rememberest that thy brother hath ought against thee; Leave there thy gift before the altar, and go thy way; FIRST BE RECONCILED to thy brother, and then come and offer thy gift.**
>
> **Matthew 5:23-24**

But SEEK YE FIRST the kingdom of God, and his righteousness; and all these things shall be added unto you.

Matthew 6:33

And why beholdest thou the mote that is in thy brother's eye, but considerest not the beam that is in thine own eye? Or how wilt thou say to thy brother, Let me pull out the mote out of thine eye; and, behold, a beam is in thine own eye? Thou hypocrite, FIRST CAST OUT THE BEAM OUT OF THINE OWN EYE; and then shalt thou see clearly to cast out the mote out of thy brother's eye.

Matthew 7:3-5

Or else how can one enter into a strong man's house, and spoil his goods, except he FIRST BIND THE STRONG MAN? and then he will spoil his house.

Matthew 12:29

Jesus said unto him, Thou shalt love the Lord thy God with all thy heart, and with all thy soul, and with all thy mind. This is the first and great commandment.

Matthew 22:37-38

Thou blind Pharisee, CLEANSE FIRST THAT WHICH IS WITHIN the cup and platter, that the outside of them may be clean also.

Matthew 23:26

The priorities of Jesus are stated throughout the Gospels.

When you are a sinner you basically choose between good and evil. As you grow in the Lord you begin to have more options. *Your choices are no longer just between good and evil, but sometimes between good and good.*

In terms of what to do there will be several good things to choose from. When you get to that point it is important that you understand the concept of priorities. Which one should I do first?

It is interesting to know the number of things Jesus said should be done first. The Scriptures above give examples of things that Jesus said should be done first. When something that is supposed to be done second is done first, many things go wrong.

Sex before Marriage or Marriage before Sex

I was recently in an African country where my host took me to a cemetery. I was amazed at the fresh graves that were gradually filling every space. At a dinner with another pastor friend, he gave me an incredible account of the number of funerals that he was conducting in his city. He told us that they had had so many funerals that pastors no longer conducted funeral services. Cell leaders had taken over this duty.

I listened in amazement. He went on and described how they no longer buried people lying down because there was no space in the cemetery. He described how they buried them vertically, standing up! I thought to myself, "In such a situation do you say, "Rest in peace," or "Stand in peace?"

What was the cause of this unprecedented wave of death? Why were so many people dying?

The answer was simple: the second thing had come before the first thing. Sex had come before marriage. When marriage comes before sex, these things ideally do not occur. Sex is supposed to be experienced only after marriage. In that country, sex is an experience occurring largely outside the context of marriage.

This is just one example of how many complicated problems occur because priorities get mixed up.

For an in-depth study of the priorities of Jesus, see my book "Proton".

Furthermore, by these few pages, my son, be admonished because of making many books there is no end

Chapter 15

Jesus, How Much Time Do We Have?

What is the time according to God's clock?

There are three times that are running simultaneously. These are "*my* time", "*your* time" and "*the* time".

Then Jesus said unto them, My time is not yet come: but your time is alway ready.

John 7:6

Take a look at your watch right now. In the natural that is your time. Take a look at some one else's watch. That is *his* time. But what is *the* time?

In real life, every watch has a slightly different time. My watch is usually set a few minutes fast to help me overcome the spirit of lateness. Other people have more accurate watches.

This phenomenon gives rise to a multitude of different times for everyone.

In the spirit realm, we all have different times. My time is different from your time. That is why Jesus said, "My time is not yet come but your time is always ready."

A few years ago, Princess Diana shocked the world by making a sudden and tragic exit. No one expected her to die when she did. No one expected her to die on the Sunday morning that she died.

A week before she died, if you had asked me, "What is the time?" I would have said, "It is Sunday morning, and time for church". If you had asked her the same question she would probably have answered, "It is another Sunday morning; and a few days before I go to be with my boyfriend in France". *Merzee*! But the time was actually seven days to her death. Unfortunately she didn't know it.

On the Saturday before she died, she was having dinner with her Egyptian boyfriend in Paris. If someone had asked you, "What time is it?" you might have said, "It is eight o'clock." If someone had asked her she may have said, "It is Saturday night, and a time of lovemaking and dreaming of a better future." But she was wrong; the real time for her was a couple of hours before the end. She was also one week closer to her funeral.

"*My* time" speaks of where I am in the timetable of *my* life. "*Your* time", speaks of where you are in the timetable of "*your* life", and "*the* time", speaks of where we are in *God's* overall timetable.

Unknown to many people, this earthly life is very time-related. Every instruction or opportunity is time-related. Hear this and hear it very well: every instruction that God has given to you has an invisible timer. A countdown begins the moment God speaks to you. The available time to perform that duty reduces with every passing hour. Many think they are just biding time and will take God seriously later. Do not be deceived! The expiry date of your grace period is fast approaching.

Like I said, Princess Diana might have been planning for her wedding. What she didn't know was that she was not far from the night of her exitus. She was oblivious to the fact that she was to be the subject of the largest funeral of all time. She didn't know the time. Do you know the time? Do we know the time?

If God has told you to do some work, the clock has begun to tick. A time will come when you will no longer be able to fulfil that instruction.

Sometimes God speaks to you: *"Finance my Kingdom."* Perhaps that comes along with a five-year period wherein you can obey Him. Perhaps He tells you: *"Go out as a missionary."* Maybe that instruction has a ten-year lease.

Some people spend eight years of that period doing other things and then in the last two years, attempt to obey God. But their time is almost up. Nothing effective can be done in the remaining two years.

One day, God is going to remove the element of time from our lives. This has been prophesied in the book of Revelation where He swore that there would no longer be time. But until then, everything we have to do is very much related to a ticking clock.

Dear Christian, if you think you have forever to please Him you are living in the highest kind of deception.

And sware by him that liveth for ever and ever, who created heaven, and the things that therein are, and the earth, and the things that therein are, and the sea, and the things which are therein, that there should be time no longer:

Revelation 10:6

To every thing there is a season, and a time to every purpose under the heaven:

Ecclesiastes 3:1

I read a book in which the author said, "Write the books you intend to write and write them now." He continued, "At another stage of your life, you will not write the same things you would have written then." How true that is. Perhaps if I were to write the books I wrote some years ago now, I would not write them in the same way today.

Five More Lives

Once, my children were playing on their play station. There was this creature that was making its way through a jungle with all sorts of amazing traps and ambushes. Gigantic wheels would appear and roll over their player. Deep ridges would appear into which the player would fall. Eagles flew over trying to kill the player. As I watched, my son's player was suddenly destroyed by a huge animal, which came from nowhere.

Then I said, "Oh, sorry, that is the end of the game. You've lost your player."

But he answered "Oh, don't worry I have five more lives. The game is not over at all."

The computer games of our world have deceived us into thinking that we have multiple lives. We have nothing but one life and one death. The clock is ticking and opportunities are passing by.

There will even be a time when you will hear the Word of God but will not be able to repent. In the book of John, Jesus said, "Do not say that there are yet four months." In other words do not give yourself extra time. This is the time of the harvest. It is time to respond now.

Say not ye, There are yet four months, and then cometh harvest? behold, I say unto you, Lift up your eyes, and look on the fields; for they are white already to harvest.

John 4:35

Gordon Lindsay, a man of God, who built Bible schools and churches in the sixties, wrote this powerful poem. It depicts the life of a young man who was offered the opportunity to get involved in the harvest. He procrastinated until he was too old to obey God. He never intended to disregard the call of God. But before he realized, his life was over.

Read this poem by Gordon Lindsay. I believe it will bless your heart:

Sunrise and skies are fair
A day begins without a care
A day for joy, a day for leisure
A day for thrills, a day for pleasure
Youth is merry and young, youth is gay
The great reaper is far away

But there is a call, 'tis the master's voice
I need you today, may I be your choice
A harvest is waiting and the fields are white
Will you join the reapers in the morning bright
Awake oh youth to the heavenly vision
Because multitudes,multitudes are in the Valley of Decision

The morning sun high above the earth
A cry of distress in the midst of mirth
Heathen are born and heathen are dying
Is there none to hear them crying?
"Oh yes," said the youth, count me as one
To help in this harvest till the day is done
Yet he lingered on for a little more fun

High sun, high noon
You'll be hearing from me soon.
I've married a wife, I've property to see
Five yoke of oxen acquired by me
I'll soon heed the call, I'll join the band
Ready to give the reapers a hand
But he carried on he had a bargain in hand

Afternoon sun and afternoon light
The golden ore hastened its flight
Conscience still hard memories daunted
Wealth, he had acquired, yet more was wanted
Many were the possessions he proudly flaunted
Houses and barns, lands and farms
Streams and ponds, stocks and bonds
Chickens and hogs, forest and logs
Crops and flack, meadows and haystacks
Orchards and berries, vineyards and cherries

Day was waxing, day was waning
Still the rich man was entertaining
For a sinister voice had spoken and said
On with the fun, on with the dance
Go ahead and make merry while you have the chance
You're a man of the times, you're ten feet tall
He saw time yet for the call
So a little more jolly and a little more fun
And the hours slipped away until there were none

Sunrise to sun fall
The day was wasting on the western wall
Hands still busy with a thousand things
As evening descends and curfew brings
The day had faded into twilight red
As multitudes hasten to join the dead

"I am ready", "I am ready" said the man at last
But shaking hands could not hold fast
His hair unnoticed had turned to gray
Still he thought it was yesterday
Alas, harvest past, it was too late
To save those who had gone to a Christless grave

Where is the silver and where is the gold?
Where are the possessions to another soul?
Where are the sheep that grazed the hill?
And where are the cattle that drank from the river?
Where are the barns that were filled with plenty?
And where are the thoroughbreds one hundred and twenty?
Where are the heirlooms? Where are the treasures?
Where is the laughter? Where are the pleasures?
Where are the porters? Where is the wine?
Where are the delicacies? And the dinners that are so fine?

Sun sunk low. And night descended
The summer is gone, the harvest is ended
O for a chance for time extended!!
A wasted life was never intended!!
Sun fall and noon rise
What is left of the rich man's prize?

Go out to the valley to yonder hill
And see the marble standing still
Treasures were offered in heaven
But he took instead
The cold reward of the unsaved dead!

And what of us who live today?
This is our home let us not stay!!
A call to the harvest till it shall end
Work now, work fast, and reap my friend
New dawn and sunrise
Till the faithful the master will give the prize.

Furthermore, by these few pages, my son, be admonished
because of making many books there is no end

Chapter 16

Jesus' Variations from the Norm

Jesus answered and said unto them, YE DO ERR, NOT KNOWING THE SCRIPTURES, nor the power of God.

Matthew 22:29

You must have heard the saying: "There is an exception to every rule." Whether this is true or not, Jesus introduced numerous scriptural exceptions to well-accepted principles. A failure to understand these exceptions led the Pharisees to vehemently oppose Christ. A lack of knowledge of the whole Scripture made them so right that they became wrong.

For example, the saying: "Physician heal thyself", is a well-accepted saying. It is true and must be practised all the time.

A physician's remedy, if worth anything, must first work on the physician himself. It could be that the physician's potion is poisonous and a good place to test it is on the physician himself. But Jesus introduced a biblical exception.

He responded to that demand by saying that a prophet is not without honour except in his own country. This means there are occasions when the physician's potion does not work. That is, in his home. In this case, "Physician, heal thyself", does not apply. Jesus used one Scripture to draw the bigger picture.

But Jesus said unto them, A prophet is not without honour, but in his own country, and among his own kin, and in his own house.

Mark 6:4

Exceptions to Keeping Bad Company

On another occasion, Jesus was accused of spending a lot of time fellowshipping with sinners (Luke 5:29-35). The Pharisees were not comfortable with a religious leader who was so at ease in the midst of well-known criminals. They confronted Him with this well-accepted divine principle "Bad company ruins good morals".

Jesus knew this principle but He knew a little more. He knew the biblical exception and He told them, "They that are whole need not a physician, but they that are sick. I came not to call the righteous but sinners to repentance."

And Jesus answering said unto them, They that are whole need not a physician; but they that are sick. I came not to call the righteous, but sinners to repentance.

Luke 5:31-32

Exceptions to Fasting

Almost every biblical rule has biblical exceptions and variations. Jesus was criticized about His disciples not fasting. Fasting is a well-accepted biblical practice. Jesus Himself fasted and never spoke against fasting. Then why were His disciples not fasting? Why did it seem that He was going against a well-accepted scriptural norm? How could He violate something that was unquestionably a good spiritual activity?

This was because, He knew a biblical exception to the rule which the Pharisees and Sadducees did not know. He said to them "Can you make the children of the bride chamber fast when the bridegroom is with them?" By this saying, Jesus introduced a biblical exception to the rule based on divine timing. He explained that there was a time when it was not appropriate to fast even though fasting is a good thing.

And he said unto them, Can ye make the children of the bridechamber fast, while the s bridegroom is with them?

Luke 5:34

When you walk with God, you will need to know not only the biblical principles but the biblical exceptions and variations to the rules. Otherwise you will become a New Testament Pharisee.

Error sets in when we know the Scripture without the power or the power without the Scriptures. Both are needed to keep us on the path of righteousness.

Jesus answered and said unto them, Ye do err, not knowing the scriptures, nor the power of God.

Matthew 22:29

In my walk with God, I have found that many things that were right became wrong when the Lord was not leading me there.

Exceptions to Prayer

Prayer is good but unbelievably there is a time when it is not a good thing to pray. It may be time to preach or time to rest and you may be in prayer. The well-accepted biblical rule that we should pray without ceasing has variations and exceptions sometimes based on timing.

In the Garden of Gethsemane, Jesus urged His disciples to pray. But at a point, He urged them to sleep. In other words, don't bother to pray any more, just sleep!

And he cometh unto the disciples, and findeth them asleep, and saith unto Peter, What, could ye not watch with me one hour? Watch and pray, that ye enter not into temptation: the spirit indeed is willing, but the flesh is weak. Then cometh he to his disciples, and saith unto them, Sleep on now, and take your rest:...

Matthew 26: 40,41,45

God is not a book. The Bible is not a god. The Bible is not God. The Bible contains the principles, the rules and the

Scriptures. It takes a personal and intimate relationship with God to stay close to God. The Pharisees were sticklers for the rules and principles they had found. Because they did not know God, they thought God was a principle or a rule. Jesus showed repeatedly that knowing God was more than knowing rules and principles. God is the author of these rules and laws.

Exceptions to Preaching and Teaching

There are times God has showed me principles from His Word. For instance, He has led me to focus on preaching, teaching and healing.   As I carried on emphasizing church planting and evangelism based on the Scriptures that I understood, I found the Lord leading me to do things that I had formerly disregarded. The Lord warned me to follow Him and not to become a Pharisee who was so bent on the laws and principles he had learnt.

The same Jesus whose last words were, "Go into the world and preach the gospel," is the same Jesus who said, "When I was hungry, you did not feed me. When I was sick you did not visit. When I was in prison, you never thought of me."

Then shall the righteous answer him, saying, Lord, when saw we thee an hungred, and fed thee? or thirsty, and gave thee drink? When saw we thee a stranger, and took thee in? or naked, and clothed thee? Or when saw we thee sick, or in prison, and came unto thee? And the King shall answer and say unto them, Verily I say unto you, Inasmuch as ye have done it unto one of the least of these my brethren, ye have done it unto me.

Matthew 25:37-40

Visiting prisoners is not the same as planting a church. Caring for the sick is not evangelism. It is a biblical variation from my long-standing view of the work of God.

How quickly we become Pharisees filled with self-righteousness when we are so sure we are doing the right thing. A deeper understanding of Jesus' Words will reveal what it means to walk with God.

Exceptions to Sabbath Activities

When Jesus was criticized about His disciples plucking corn and eating it on the Sabbath day, He once again brought an exception and variation to the law. He pointed out how David had eaten the shew bread with his followers. He then gave another principle which the Pharisees did not know, "The Son of man is Lord also of the Sabbath."

For the Son of man is Lord even of the sabbath day.

Matthew 12:8

This means that God is the creator of the rules and laws and He is higher than them.

Exceptions to Poverty

Once, Jesus asked His disciples to go on evangelism without making financial provision. He told them not to bother about taking extra money or supplies.

And he said unto them, Take nothing for your journey, neither staves, nor scrip, neither bread, neither money; neither have two coats apiece.

Luke 9:3

However, not so long after He sent them again and this time He told them to take enough money, clothes and supplies.

Then said he unto them, But now, he that hath a purse, let him take it, and likewise his scrip: and he that hath no sword, let him sell his garment, and buy one.

Luke 22:36

Once again, you learn the principle of not equating God to a rule that you have learnt. Following God is more than following a couple of learnt rules. If all we needed were rules, then we would no longer need God Himself. There is no particular rule that can replace our relationship with God. This reality has made me conscious of my need to follow the Lord and to be close to Him personally. None of the things I have learned can replace a personal day to day walk with the Lord. What I perceive as being right today may be wrong for tomorrow.

Jesus Is the Truth

No particular rule, doctrine or principle is truth; Jesus himself is the truth. He said, "I am the way the truth and the life."

Jesus saith unto him, I am...the truth...

John 14:6

Following Jesus closely is our best chance of abiding in truth. Today, it is easy to see that the Pharisees were incredibly estranged from truth. They were far from the truth because they were far from God Himself.

What about us? How far are we from God? Perhaps we also have some old principles that we cherish. We think that by following these rules we will be following God. Can you see how many movements and churches become distant from the Lord?   Many churches have rejected the current commands of God in order to keep their traditions.

And he said unto them, Full well ye reject the commandment of God, that ye may keep your own tradition.

Mark 7:9

This is the number one cause of backsliding among religious people. May God help us all!

Furthermore, by these few pages, my son, be admonished because of making many books there is no end